The Dare

Classroom Questions

A SCENE BY SCENE TEACHING GUIDE

Amy Farrell

SCENE BY SCENE
ENNISKERRY, IRELAND

Copyright © 2017 by Scene by Scene.

Without limiting the rights under copyright, this book is sold subject to the condition that it shall not, by way of trade or otherwise be lent, resold, hired out, reproduced, stored on or introduced into a retrieval system, or transmitted, in any form or by any means (electronic, mechanical, photocopying, recording or otherwise), or otherwise circulated, without the publisher's prior consent, in any form other than that in which it is published and without a similar condition, including this condition, being imposed on the subsequent publisher.

All rights reserved. No part of this publication may be recorded or transmitted in any form or by any means electronic, mechanical, photocopying, recording or otherwise without the proper consent of the publisher.

The publisher reserves the right to change, without notice, at any time, the specification of this product, whether by change of materials, colours, format, text revision or any other characteristic.

Scene by Scene
Enniskerry
Wicklow, Ireland.
www.scenebysceneguides.com

The Dare Classroom Questions by Amy Farrell.
ISBN 978-1-910949-65-8

Contents

Chapter One	1
Chapter Two	4
Chapter Three	8
Chapter Four	12
Chapter Five	16
Chapter Six	20
Chapter Seven	26
Chapter Eight	32
Chapter Nine	36
Chapter Ten	41
Chapter Eleven	48
Further Questions	54

Chapter One

Summary

One day in the school holidays, the speaker comes home to an empty house, which is odd as his mother is usually home.

He wishes his big brother, Pete, was there to talk to.

He is watching television when his dad comes home. He wonders where Danny's mother is.

By eight o'clock his dad is starting to get worried. He phones a few of her friends and wants to phone more. He does not though, as Danny's mam went out like this once before and was annoyed that Danny's dad was looking for her, asking could she not have a life of her own.

Danny's dad sends him up to bed at half nine, but he does not go to sleep.

He hears a car and the doorbell rings. Danny watches from the top of the stairs. His mother is at the door, flanked by a policeman and policewoman on either side.

Questions

1. When did 'it' start?

2. Who is Luke Kennedy?

3. What is strange when the narrator arrives home?

4. Who is Pete?
   Why isn't he home?

5. Why does the speaker wish Pete was there?

6. Why does the speaker kneel down under the windowsill?

7. Is Danny's dad as funny as he thinks he is?

8. What are your first impressions of Danny's dad?

9. Why does Danny's dad start to get worried at eight o'clock?

10. What stops Danny's dad from phoning some more people?
    What does this suggest about Danny's parents' relationship?

11. Why doesn't Danny argue about going to bed?

12. Does Danny go to sleep?
    Would you, in his position?

13. Who brings Danny's mam home?
    What, do you think, is going on here?

14. What gets your attention, in this opening chapter?
    What makes you want to read on?

15. Based on the information you receive in this chapter, what are Danny's parents like?
    Use examples to support the points that you make.

16. Do Danny's family sound close to you?
    Do they get on well together?

Chapter Two

Summary

Danny's dad asks what has happened.

The police ask him to confirm that Danny's mam is his wife.

Danny's dad is angry, wanting answers. The policeman tells him to calm down, saying they will explain it all to him.

Danny worries about Pete, as he has not phoned in a couple of days. He thinks that something has happened to him, and that is why his mam went to the police station.

Danny goes downstairs, but cannot overhear the conversation properly.

He picks the policeman's helmet up off the floor and puts it on.

His dad and the police come into the hallway, to Danny's embarrassment.

His dad sends him upstairs, but he does not go into his room, and stays by the banister.

He overhears his dad asking the police to get in touch if they have any news and saying it is a terrible thing.

They say they will need to speak to his wife again the next day.

After his mam goes to bed, Danny's dad comes up and talks to him. He tells him that there was an accident, that a little boy ran out in front of Danny's mother's car and she knocked him down. He is currently in hospital.

Danny's dad tells him that everything will be fine and that he is not to bother his mother in the morning.

Danny thinks about the little boy and feels that nothing will be the same at home ever again.

Questions

1. How does Danny's dad react to seeing his wife accompanied by police at the door?

2. Describe the policeman and policewoman.

3. Why does the policewoman ask if they can sit down?

4. Is Danny's dad concerned about his wife?

5. Why does Danny start to worry about Pete?

6. Why didn't Danny speak to Pete the other night on the phone?
   Does this tell you anything about Danny's family?

7. Why does Danny go downstairs?

8. Describe the policeman's helmet.

9. How does Danny feel when he is caught wearing the helmet?
   How would you feel in his position?

10. What does Danny do when he is sent to his room?

11. What does Danny overhear his dad saying to the police?
    What could be going on here, do you think?

12. How has Danny's dad's demeanour changed by the time the police leave?

13. Why was Danny's mother with the police?
    What is your response to this?
    Did you see this coming or are you taken by surprise?

14. How is the little boy?

15. Does Danny's dad do a good job of reassuring Danny that everything will be fine?
    Refer to the text in your answer.

16. How is Danny feeling as the chapter ends?

17. How would you feel if you were Danny's mother?

18. What is the mood like as the chapter ends?

Chapter Three

Summary

Danny's mam stays in bed the next morning. His dad tells him to stay out of her way, which he does, as he is afraid to see her.

Danny goes upstairs to get his book. His mother bursts into tears when she sees him. His dad gives out to him and sends him outside.

He comes home close to six o'clock, to an empty house.

Alice Kennedy, a neighbour, knocks on the door. She says Danny's dad phoned her, thinking he might be hungry. He is reluctant to leave, but he goes with her.

He likes holding her hand, but lets go before they go into the house, not wanting Luke to see.

Mrs Kennedy's boyfriend, Benjamin Benson, is in the kitchen with Luke. Mr Benson chats to Danny and asks him to taste the mushroom sauce.

Danny tells Luke he did not ask to come, but Luke says he does not care who his mother invites for dinner, it is still his dad's house.

Danny says he will have a glass of Coke. Mr Benson says it rots the teeth, but is his addiction. When he talks about addictions, Danny does not know if he is joking or not. Mrs Kennedy laughs, so Danny assumes he is joking.

Danny stops himself from laughing along with Mr Benson, as Luke looks like he is ready to kill someone.

Mrs Kennedy mentions David, Luke's father. Luke says that it is his father's house, something that Mrs Kennedy contradicts.

Danny tries to imagine what life would be like without his dad or mam, and loses his appetite. He is on the verge of tears, which causes Luke to laugh at him.

Mrs. Kennedy brings Danny into the living room so he can take a quiet moment.

Questions

1. Where is Danny's mam the next morning?

2. Why does Danny stay out of his mam's way?

3. What does Danny's mother do when she sees him? Can you explain her reaction here?

4. How does Danny's father react to his wife's tears? Is he fair to Danny here?

5. Why can't Danny concentrate on his book? What does he do instead?

6. Who knocks on Danny's door that evening? What is she doing there?

7. Does Danny want to go with Alice Kennedy? How do you know this?

8. Who is Benjamin Benson? What does he look like?

9. Does Luke get on well with Benjamin Benson? What makes you say this?

10. What are your first impressions of Mr Benson?

11. Is Luke glad to see Danny?

12. Does Luke get on well with his mother?
    What makes you say this?

13. Do Mr Benson and Luke's mother get on well together?
    Explain your point of view, using examples from the story to support your ideas.

14. Why does Danny stop himself from laughing at Mr Benson?

15. What is Luke's problem?

16. Who is David?

17. Why doesn't Danny eat his dinner?

18. Why is Danny on the verge of tears?

19. How does Luke react to seeing that Danny is close to tears?

20. Why does Mrs Kennedy bring Danny into the living room?

21. Does Luke sound like somebody you would like to be friends with?
    Give reasons for your answer.

22. Are Danny's parents coping well with his mother's accident?
    Refer to the story to support the points that you make.

Chapter Four

Summary

Later that night, Danny's dad phones and asks that he stay overnight at Mrs Kennedy's. Danny's heart sinks as he wants to go home.

Danny's parents are at the hospital as his mother is not well. Mrs Kennedy takes the phone and assures Danny's dad that Danny will be fine with her.

Mrs Kennedy makes up the top bunk in Luke's room for Danny. Once they are in bed, Luke calls Mr Benson an idiot. He plans to tell his dad about him when he goes to stay with him.

Luke asks Danny what is going on at his house. When Danny says there is nothing going on, Luke says he heard that Danny's mam got drunk and knocked someone down and killed them.

Danny says this is not true, but Luke replies that he heard it from his mam. Danny adds that his mam did not kill anybody, but they are in a coma and it is not hopeful.

Mrs Kennedy looks in on the boys. Luke asks if Danny is staying the following night too. This startles Danny, he wonders how long this will go on for.

Mrs Kennedy tells them that she does not know yet.

After Luke falls asleep, Danny whispers that his mam was not drunk.

Questions

1. Danny speaks "nervously" into the telephone.
   Why is he feeling this way?

2. Does Danny want to stay in Mrs Kennedy's house?
   Would you, if you were him?

3. Where are Danny's parents?
   What is your response to this?

4. Why does Alice Kennedy take the phone from Danny?

5. Is Mrs Kennedy a good friend of Danny's parents, do you think?

6. Where will Danny sleep?

7. What does Danny see when he looks in through his bedroom window?
   What does it make him think of?

8. What does Luke call Mr Benson at bedtime?
   Why does he feel this way about him?

9. Do you feel sorry for Luke?
   Explain your view.

10. Danny tells Luke there is nothing going on at his house.
    What makes him lie like this, do you think?

11. What has Luke heard about what happened?
    Who did he hear this from?
    What is your response to this?

12. Why is Danny alarmed at the thought of staying another night at the Kennedys'?

13. Why does Danny whisper that his mother was not drunk? Explain why this is important.

14. Describe Danny's character, based on what you have read so far.

15. Describe Luke Kennedy, based on what you have read so far.

16. Are the boys alike? Explain your answer.

17. Do you think that Danny's parents are doing enough to care for him at the moment?
    Include examples in your answer.

Chapter Five

Summary

Danny's dad says his mam was not drunk when she knocked the boy down. He says that although it was not Danny's mam's fault, she feels responsible.

A witness says Danny's mam was not even driving fast, but the little boy ran out into the road without looking.

Danny's dad tells him to go outside. When he gets on his bike, he sees a red-haired girl watching him from behind a tree. He stares back as he cycles past her.

He gets a puncture and has to wheel his bike home. He comes home via Parker Grove, the road where the accident happened.

He overhears a neighbour asking Andy's parents how he is doing. They reply that he is no worse.

Samantha, Andy's mother, wishes that he would respond to them, but so far, he has not. She starts to cry.

The woman asks how Sarah is coping. Samantha says Sarah will not talk about it with them.

Danny realises the women are staring at him and explains that he was trying to find the puncture in his tyre. They stare at him as he walks off.

When he gets back to his street, the girl with red hair is waiting there. He knows he has to talk to her.

Danny accuses her of watching him and she does not deny it. He realises she is Sarah, Andy's sister. They have spent the day spying on each other's family, and are finally getting to speak to each other.

Questions

1. Was Danny's mam drunk when the accident happened, according to Danny's dad?

2. His dad is reading a spaghetti packet.
   What does this tell you?

3. Why is Danny's mam so upset, according to his dad?

4. According to the witness, what happened?
   Does it sound like it was Danny's mam's fault to you?

5. Why was the little boy there?

6. Describe the girl Danny sees watching him.

7. How does he respond to the girl's stares?
   What would you do here?

8. Why does Danny wheel his bike home?

9. What route home does Danny take?

10. How does he find Andy's house?

11. What does he learn about Andy's condition?

12. Why does Samantha start to cry?

13. How is Sarah coping with Andy's condition?
    Who is Sarah, do you think?

14. How do the women react to Danny when they spot him?

15. What is Danny's excuse for being there?
    Is this a good excuse, do you think?

16. How does Danny know the red-haired girl is waiting for him?

17. Why doesn't Danny normally like talking to girls?

18. How does the girl respond when Danny accuses her of watching him?

19. What does Danny realise about this girl?

20. What does Danny compare himself and Sarah to?

21. Are you surprised that they have met like this?

22. Would you have gone to Andy's house, in Danny's position?
    Give reasons for your answer.

23. Why, do you think, has Sarah turned up here?

24. What, do you think, will happen next?

Chapter Six

Summary

The following Saturday, Danny is waiting for Sarah in the park. He is happy to see her.

Sarah thought he might have changed his mind about meeting her. She was nearly late as her mother got mad when she would not go to the hospital to see her brother.

Danny asks if Andy will get better, but Sarah does not know the answer. Danny assures her he will, a statement that annoys Sarah.

She asks Danny how he knew who she was when she came to his house, but he does not really know. She came to see his mam.

Danny is afraid Sarah will start crying, but she does not.

She says what happened is not Danny's mam's fault, but hers.

Danny spots Luke Kennedy, with his mother and Benjamin Benson, walking towards them. Mrs Kennedy is surprised to see Danny with a girl. She asks for an introduction, but Sarah says they are not friends, that she was just sitting there.

Mr Benson suggests that Danny was chatting her up, to his embarrassment. Luke is annoyed because Danny told him that he was busy and could not go out today.

Sarah stands up to leave. Danny wants to know what she has to say about the accident. He asks her to wait, but Luke interrupts, saying they will go for a cycle.

Luke shouts goodbye after Sarah and she stops and stares at him. Mr Benson apologises for chasing her away.

Danny stays out later than usual that night. When he gets in, his dad asks him where he was. His mam has gone to bed. This bothers Danny, as she was in bed when he left earlier that afternoon.

His dad says Danny would have seen her if he had come home on time. He tells Danny he should talk to his mam.

Danny's dad has invited his grandparents over next week for Danny's birthday. They will have a family dinner.

Danny is not sure whether he wants a party, but his dad says it will be fun.

Danny is thinking about whether he will get to see Sarah again. He wants to find out why she said everything is her fault. Then he can tell his mam, so she will not be upset and things can go back to normal.

Questions

1. Where do Danny and Sarah meet on Saturday?

2. Why is he reading *David Copperfield*?
   Does this tell you anything about him?

3. How does Danny feel about seeing Sarah?

4. Why was Sarah nearly late?

5. How often do her family visit Andy?
   What do you think of this?

6. Why is Danny reluctant to ask how Andy is?

7. Is Andy going to get better?
   How must his family be feeling?

8. What makes Sarah look angry?
   Why does she react like this, do you think?

9. What does Danny decide to do in future?
   What does this suggest about Danny?

10. How did Danny know who Sarah was when she came to his house?
    Do you understand why she came?
    Would you do something like this, in her position?

11. How have things been for Sarah recently?

12. Does Sarah blame Danny's mam for Andy's accident?

13. Who does Danny spot walking towards them?
    Is he glad to see them? Why/why not?

14. How does Mrs Kennedy respond to seeing Danny with a girl?

15. "...I'd grown an inch and a half over the last three months, not that anyone had noticed except me."
    What insight does this statement give you into Danny and his life?

16. What stops Danny from introducing Sarah to Mrs Kennedy?

17. Should he be talking to Sarah, in your view?
    Give a reason for your answer.

18. How does Sarah get them out of this situation?

19. Why is Luke annoyed with Danny?

20. Sarah leaves suddenly.
    How does Danny feel about this?
    How does this affect the story?

21. Why does Luke interrupt Danny?

22. What does Luke shout after Sarah?
    What does he mean by this?
    Why is he acting this way, do you think?

23. Have Danny's neighbours chased Sarah away here?

24. What is your response to this episode?

25. What excuse does Danny give for staying out late?

26. Why wasn't Danny's dad worried?
    What does this tell you about how things are in Danny's house?

27. Where is Danny's mam?
    How does Danny react to this?
    Can you explain his reaction?

28. How have Danny's parents spent the evening?

29. What does Danny's dad want him to do?

30. What has Danny's dad planned for his birthday?
    Are you surprised by this?

31. Would you want a party, if you were Danny?

32. What is Danny really thinking about as his dad talks to him?

33. Why is Danny determined to discover Sarah's secret?

34. What would you do next, if you were Danny?

35. What is the atmosphere like in Danny's house at the moment?

36. Why have we seen so little of Danny's mam? What impression are you forming of her?

Chapter Seven

Summary

It is Danny's birthday dinner. His grandparents and the Kennedys have come over. Danny's mam is not there. Benjamin is keeping the conversation alive.

Benjamin talks about his father being a conscientious objector during the war, something that does not impress Danny's grandfather.

The only presents Danny got are a jumper from his grandmother and some money from his grandfather. Mrs Kennedy has a book for him.

Danny's dad gives him a card from Pete. Danny is relieved that his brother has not forgotten him.

Danny's dad says they will take Danny out over the weekend and get him something special then, but Luke says it does not count if it is not your birthday.

They have not started dinner as Danny's mother is not back yet. Mrs Kennedy suggests going to look for her, but Benjamin warns against walking around the area late at night.

Danny's dad is annoyed that his wife is half an hour late and says they will go ahead and eat.

Danny's mam arrives at a quarter to nine, while they are eating his birthday cake.

Russell, Danny's dad, tells her that it is not good enough, her arriving late like this. She snaps at him and tells him to shut up.

He says that she cannot have any dinner because she is late. She finds this ridiculous, but he is serious.

It is very tense. Rachel, Danny's mam, says she is sorry. She has tears in her eyes. She gets angry with Russell, saying he does not have the weight of nearly killing a child on his conscience.

He points out that it was an accident and that she should think about her own kids.

She shakes her head, saying there is only one who matters, and Danny knows she means Andy.

As Danny is putting the bins out later that night, Sarah calls to him. She has come back. He is glad to see her.

She asks him to visit her brother in hospital with her on Monday. He hesitates, not sure if he wants to see what his mother has done.

He asks Sarah why she said it was all her fault, but before she answers him, Danny's dad comes out looking for him.

Sarah says she will explain everything at the hospital on Monday.

Questions

1. What is taking place as this chapter begins?

2. Does it sound like a fun get-together so far?
   Use examples from the story to support the points you make.

3. How did Benjamin's father spend the war?

4. What are your first impressions of Danny's grandfather?
   Give reasons for your answer.

5. What has Danny been given for his birthday?
   Can you explain why this happened?
   How would you feel about this, if you were Danny?

6. Do Danny's grandparents get on well together?

7. What present has Pete sent?

8. How does Danny feel when he sees Pete has sent him something?

9. Where is Pete at the moment?

10. Was Danny's dad pleased to hear from Pete the last time he called?
    Why/why not?

CLASSROOM QUESTIONS

11. Why did Danny say that he did not get anything for his birthday?
    How does his father plan to make it up to him?

12. Luke says you have to get a present on your birthday for it to count.
    Do you agree with him?

13. Why haven't the guests been given their dinner yet?

14. What suggestion does Mrs Kennedy make about finding Danny's mam?
    How does Benjamin respond to this suggestion?
    Does this tell you anything about the area where they live?

15. How is Danny's dad feeling?
    How does he show his emotions?

16. What does Danny's dad decide they should do?
    How would you feel if you were Danny?

17. When does Danny's mam arrive home?

18. How does Russell (Danny's dad) react when she comes in?
    What makes him behave like this?

19. How does Rachel speak to Russell here?
    What is your response to this?

20. Danny's dad says that Rachel cannot have any dinner.
    How does she respond to this?
    What is your response?

21. How does Belinda, Rachel's mother, get brought into the argument?
How would you feel, in her position?

22. What makes this a tense moment in the story?

23. 'I've had enough of this, Rachel'
Is Russell understanding and sympathetic towards his wife?
Does he treat her fairly here?

24. "This was who she was now, I realised."
How is Rachel behaving?
Can you explain her behaviour?
Why is her behaviour difficult for Danny to understand?

25. Danny's dad tells Rachel to think about the kids for once.
Is this a fair comment?
What is your response to the way he speaks to her here?

26. Danny says that Pete is his mother's favourite.
What is your response to this?
Do you feel sorry for Danny here?

27. "...I knew the only kid who mattered was Andy."
Why does Rachel feel this way?
How would you feel, if you were Danny?

28. Why can't Sarah stay very long?

29. What does Sarah ask Danny to do for her?

30. Why does he hesitate before answering?

31. What question does Danny ask her?
    Why doesn't she answer?

32. What does Sarah promise Danny?

33. Would you go with her on Monday? Why/why not?

34. Describe the atmosphere in Danny's house at this point.

35. How has the car accident affected Danny's parents and their relationship?

36. What is the mood like as the chapter ends?

37. Danny's birthday party takes place in this chapter.
    What age do you think he is?
    Give reasons for your answer.

38. Imagine you are Danny. Write the diary entry for the day of your birthday party. Mention what happened and how you felt about it.

Chapter Eight

Summary

Danny goes to visit Andy with Sarah. She is glad he came.

Andy looks like he is fast asleep, connected to lots of hospital equipment.

Sarah asks Danny to say hello to her brother, and feeling awkward, he does so.

Danny tells her about the time Pete was taken to hospital when his appendix burst.

Sarah sits in an armchair, covering her face. She begins by saying it was supposed to be a game, and explains how Andy was doing a dare on the afternoon he was knocked down by Rachel's car.

Sarah blames herself for the accident. Danny starts to get angry, annoyed that his mother is blaming herself for something that is not her fault.

They hear Sarah's parents' voices and she tells Danny to hide under the bed. He does not want to, but slides under just in time.

Samantha, Andy's mother, blames Rachel for the accident. She is annoyed that the police will not be pressing charges. She calls Rachel a maniac and is indignant that she is getting away with Andy's accident.

Unable to listen to this, Danny springs out from beneath the hospital bed. He blames Sarah for the accident, before turning and running away.

Questions

1. Describe Andy and the hospital equipment he is connected to.

2. Describe Andy's appearance.

3. Why does Danny feel awkward and embarrassed?

4. Why was Pete in hospital once?

5. "I don't know what mam would have done if he hadn't got better, because he's her favourite."
How do Danny's words here make you feel?

6. "It was only supposed to be a game"
What does Sarah tell Danny about?

7. Why did Andy run out into the road that afternoon?

8. Is the whole thing Sarah's fault?
Give reasons for your answer.

9. Why does Danny start to get angry?
Do you understand what makes him feel this way?

10. Why does Sarah tell Danny to get under the bed?
How would you feel, in his position?

11. What have the police decided about the accident?
How does this make you feel?

12. What does Samantha say about Danny's mother?
    What is your response to these comments?

13. Does she mean everything she says, do you think?
    What makes her say these things?

14. How does Danny react to Samantha's comments about his mother?

15. Is Danny right to blame Sarah like this?

16. Danny runs away at the end of the chapter.
    Was this the best thing to do here?
    What would you do, in his position?

17. What adds tension to this scene in the hospital room?

18. Do you feel sorry for Sarah here?
    Give reasons for your answer.

19. How would you illustrate this chapter?
    Explain your choice of images.

Chapter Nine

Summary

Later on, Danny's dad comes into his room. The police have called around. Mr and Mrs Maclean (Andy's parents) have reported Danny for trespassing in their son's hospital room.

Danny's dad does not want to believe it, but Danny admits to being there. His dad shouts at him before he can explain what happened.

Danny says that Sarah asked him to the hospital and explains how he has got to know her.

His dad says she has no business coming to their house, and asks how Danny's mother would feel if she ran into her.

Danny points out that this is not a very good choice of words, which angers his father.

His dad asks him to consider how the Macleans felt when he jumped out from underneath Andy's bed.

Danny shouts that he wishes Andy would just die. His father slaps him in the face.

Shocked, his father apologises. Danny closes his eyes and waits for his dad to leave. He does not want to live at home anymore.

An hour later, Sarah calls to the door to say sorry. She has climbed out her bedroom window to come and see him.

Danny's dad will not let her in to talk to Danny, saying they have no business being friends, that they are not helping matters. He tells her to go home.

Danny asks her to stay, but she leaves, saying she will call him.

When she leaves, Danny runs back up to his room, ignoring his dad's calls.

He looks out the window and is jealous to see Sarah talking to Luke Kennedy. They both get on Luke Kennedy's bike and he cycles away.

Danny decides he does not want to see either of them, or his parents, again. He will wait until everyone is in bed and then run away.

That night, Danny packs a change of clothes and takes some biscuits and water with him. He gets on his bike and cycles away.

Questions

1. Why does Danny's dad come into his room?

2. Why have the police called to the house?
   What is your response to this?

3. "Tell me they've got it wrong."
   How is Danny's dad feeling at this stage?

4. How does Danny feel about the incident in the hospital room?

5. How does Danny's dad react when he hears that Danny was in the hospital room?

6. Does Danny's dad listen to him?

7. What makes Danny's dad really angry?

8. How does Danny react when his dad asks him to think how Andy's parents felt when he jumped out from underneath the bed?
   Are you shocked by his reaction here?

9. How does Danny's dad react to Danny's outburst?
   What do you think of this?

10. How does Danny's dad feel about what he has just done?

CLASSROOM QUESTIONS

11. "I didn't want to live there any more."
    Explain what makes Danny feel this way.
    Do you feel sorry for Danny here?

12. If you were Danny's dad, what would you say or do to try to make things right with Danny?

13. Why does Sarah come to Danny's house?

14. 'All they think about is Andy anyway'.
    What effect is Andy's accident having on the Maclean family?

15. Why won't Danny's dad allow Sarah in?
    Is he doing the right thing here, do you think?

16. Danny's father tells Danny and Sarah that they have no business being friends.
    Is he right, in your view?

17. What does Danny do when Sarah leaves?

18. What makes Danny jealous?

19. What decision does Danny come to?

20. What does Danny take with him?

21. Has Danny thought his plan through?

22. Are you surprised that Danny runs away like this?
    What has caused him to make this decision?

23. What, do you think, will happen next?

Chapter Ten

Summary

Danny cycles to the school, hoping to hide out behind the sports hall. He cannot sleep as he forgot to bring a sleeping bag, and is afraid of something coming around the corner and killing him.

He begins to nod off as it gets bright, but decides to keep moving so as to avoid being found.

He has breakfast of a burger and chips at a fastfood restaurant. When he goes back outside, he discovers that his bike has been stolen.

Danny eats another burger and chips in the afternoon, with ice cream this time. He only has three pounds left.

He feels nervous walking around town whenever he sees the police, knowing that his dad has called them.

At four o'clock Danny spends the last of his money on a cinema ticket.

He walks around town that night and sits in the car park behind the shopping centre, near the big skips.

Thinking of his bed at home, he feels sad, but does not cry. He also feels hungry, but there is nothing he can do about it.

Every so often he dozes off, but he does not sleep properly.

He is stiff and sore when it gets bright again.

Danny decides to go to London and get a job.

Walking past a television shop, he sees his picture on the screen, but nobody stops or recognises him.

Later, he worries about how hungry, weak and tired he is. He thinks about going home, but decides against it.

He steals a hat to wear as a disguise.

By lunchtime, he is so hungry that his stomach hurts.

He is unsure how to get to London without any money. He remembers that David Copperfield walked from London to Dover on his own, so decides he can walk it.

That night he sleeps between the trees at the end of the rugby field at school. Although he sleeps for a few hours, he feels worse than ever when he wakes up.

It feels like he has been away from home for a very long time.

He has trouble standing up. His stomach hurts, he is no longer really hungry.

He spends the day walking the streets, wanting to eat. His legs are shaky.

That night, he goes to the park.

Danny wants to go home, but thinks it is too late now, after what he has done, to be allowed home.

As he is lying down, he falls and hits his arm against a tree. He cannot stand back up. Looking at his bleeding arm makes him dizzy.

Everything looks blurry and feels like it is closing in on him.

He tries to open his eyes wider, but this makes his stomach hurt more. He wants to stand up, but keeps falling, so gives up and lies on the ground.

He thinks he hears someone saying his name and assumes he is imagining it. This person picks him up. Nothing hurts anymore and Danny wonders if this is what it is like to die.

Danny wants to open his eyes, to know who saved him. He opens his eyes, but all he can say is 'Pete'. He closes his eyes and everything goes black.

Questions

1. What is Danny's first night away from home like?

2. Why can't he sleep?

3. Why doesn't he go home?

4. What makes him keep moving?

5. What does Danny have for breakfast?

6. What happens Danny's bike?
   What is your response to this?

7. What does Danny eat later that afternoon?

8. Is his money lasting well?

9. Do you think Danny is doing a good job of managing on his own?
   If you were Danny, what would you do differently?

10. What makes Danny nervous, walking around the streets in town?

11. Where does Danny go at four o'clock?

12. How does Danny spend his second night away from home?

13. What makes him feel sad?

CLASSROOM QUESTIONS • 45

14. Why does he keep thinking about food?

15. What would you do next, if you were Danny?

16. Does Danny get a good night's sleep?

17. How does Danny feel when he gets up?

18. What does Danny plan to do with his day?

19. What does Danny see on television?
    How does this make him feel?

20. How would you feel, seeing this, if you were Danny?

21. What does Danny worry about later on?

22. Why doesn't he go home?

23. How would you be feeling now, if you were Danny's mam or dad?

24. What disguise does Danny get?
    Is it difficult to get?

25. How is Danny feeling by lunchtime?

26. What is stopping Danny from going to London?

27. Where does Danny spend his third night away from home?

28. How does he feel when he wakes up?

29. "I wondered whether Dad and Mam had got used to not having me around any more."
    What does this sentence tell you about how Danny is feeling?

30. How is Danny feeling physically?

31. How does he spend the next day?

32. Where does he stay that night?

33. Why is it "too late" to go home?
    Is this really the case?

34. What happens Danny as he is about to lie down?

35. Why can't he stand up?

36. What condition is he in?

37. What makes this moment tense?

38. "...I wasn't going to get up ever again."
    What is happening Danny here?

39. What does Danny hear?

40. What does the figure do?
    What does Danny compare this sensation to?

41. Who has found Danny?
    How does this make you feel?

42. What is the mood like as this chapter ends?

43. What do you expect will happen when Danny sees his parents?

44. Does Danny manage well living on the streets?
    What should he have done differently?
    Should he have gone home instead of sleeping rough like this?

45. Write the text for the television news report covering Danny's disappearance. Try to make it sound as realistic as possible.

Chapter Eleven

Summary

Andy wakes up and asks for his mam and dad. Danny's dad gets a phonecall about it. He hugs Rachel and tells her everything is going to be alright.

Danny is just out of hospital, having spent six nights there. He was in danger of getting pneumonia and was dehydrated.

He was only given small things to eat in hospital, so was very hungry.

His whole family are together, watching over him.

He is to rest at home, so stays in bed.

Pete comes in to talk to him. He says Danny gave them all quite a fright.

Pete was in Prague when their dad phoned him to say Danny was missing. Pete came home immediately.

Danny tells Pete about walking around when he was gone, and how he did not eat and felt unwell before Pete found him.

Pete tells him he should not have run away. Danny says he had to, that Pete was not there, so does not know what it was like.

Pete says that instead of befriending Andy's sister, Danny should have been taking care of their mam.

Danny tries to argue his case, pointing out again that Pete was not there, so does not know what it was like.

Danny finds himself getting upset with Pete for going to university in Scotland.

Pete promises that Danny can visit him, if Danny promises not to do anything like this again. He asks that Danny call him instead the next time.

Danny thanks Pete for saving him.

Pete goes back to Europe.

Luke Kennedy joins Danny when they go to stay with Danny's grandparents.

That day with Sarah, Luke went with her to tell her parents that Danny was not as horrible as they thought.

Mrs Kennedy says Luke, like Danny, has not had a very good summer. Luke was supposed to spend a lot of it with his father, but it has not worked out that way.

Danny's mam is starting to look more like her old self.

Luke tells Danny that he has not seen his dad since Christmas. His dad hardly talks to him on the phone and always cancels visits with him.

Luke realises that Benjamin is not so bad and hopes to go to some matches with him when the new season starts.

Danny's mam comes into his room on the last night of the school holidays. She says she is sorry he did not have much of a summer holiday.

She says how horrible it was and how bad she felt for hurting Andy. She says she does not know how she would have coped if he had not got better.

Danny does not like his mam saying sorry to him, but she says she let him down.

She makes him promise not to do anything like running away again.

She tells him that everything is back to normal now. Danny feels the problems of the last few weeks slip away.

He picks up *David Copperfield,* and continues reading.

Questions

1. What happens out of the blue?
   Are you surprised by this development?

2. How does Danny's father respond to this news?

3. How does Danny's mother respond to this news?
   How would you feel, if you were her?

4. Why has Danny been in hospital?

5. Why was he starving in the hospital?

6. "The whole family was back together."
   What has brought Danny's family together?
   What is your response to this?

7. What have the doctors told Danny to do, now that he is back at home?

8. Was Danny very sick?
   Refer to the story to support the points you make.

9. Why does Danny feel a bit ashamed of himself?

10. Where was Pete when he heard Danny was missing?
    Are you surprised that he came home immediately?

11. What reasons does Danny give Pete for running away?
    Are they valid reasons?

12. Why does Pete think that befriending Sarah was not a good idea?
    Do you agree with him?

13. Why does Danny start getting upset with Pete?
    Is any of this Pete's fault?
    Can you explain why Danny is feeling this way?

14. What promise does Pete make Danny?
    What does he ask in return?

15. Are you surprised that Pete returns to his holiday in Europe?

16. Why did Luke cycle off with Sarah that day?
    What does this tell you about Luke?

17. Danny says that it was not long before the three of them became friends, which led to other problems.
    What, do you think, does he mean here?

18. Why hasn't Luke had a very good summer, according to Mrs Kennedy?

19. How is Danny's mam changing?

20. How do they spend their time at Gran and Granddad's house?

21. What does Danny learn about Luke's dad?

22. What has Luke decided to do about this?
    How does this make you feel?

23. How is Luke's attitude to Benjamin changing?

24. Does Benjamin work hard at his relationship with Luke? Include examples to support your answer.

25. What do Danny and his mam talk about on the last night of the summer holidays?

26. Why does Danny's mam want to give up driving? Is this an over-reaction, do you think, or understandable given the circumstances?

27. Why does Danny's mam feel that she let him down? Has she let him down in your opinion?

28. How does Danny feel after talking to his mam?

29. Do Danny and his mother have a good relationship? Explain your answer fully.

30. Is this a good ending? Give a reason for your answer.

Further Questions

1. Describe Danny's character, using examples from the text to support your ideas.
   What are his strengths?
   What are his weaknesses?
   What makes him an interesting main character?

2. Describe Danny's father's character, using examples from the text to support your ideas.
   What are his strengths?
   What are his weaknesses?

3. Describe Danny's mother's character, using examples from the text to support your ideas.
   What are her strengths?
   What are her weaknesses?

4. Describe Sarah's character, using examples from the text to support your ideas.
   What are her strengths?
   What are her weaknesses?

5. Describe Luke's character, using examples from the text to support your ideas.
   What are his strengths?
   What are his weaknesses?

CLASSROOM QUESTIONS

6. Is Benjamin Benson a funny character?
   Refer to the text to support your answer.

7. Do Danny and his father have a good relationship?
   Include examples in your answer.

8. Do Danny and his mother have a good relationship?
   Include examples in your answer.

9. Do Danny and his brother have a good relationship?
   Include examples in your answer.

10. What strengths do you see in Danny's family and their relationships with each other?

11. What weaknesses do you see in Danny's family and their relationships with each other?

12. Danny says that his brother, Pete, is his mother's favourite.
    What does this tell you about this family?
    How has feeling this way affected Danny, do you think?

13. What does this novel teach us about families?

14. Do you notice any similarities between Danny and Sarah?

15. In your opinion, who, if anyone, was to blame for Andy's accident?
    Give a reason for your answer.

16. Both Rachel (Danny's mother) and Samantha (Andy's mother) hold Rachel responsible for the accident.
    What insight does this give you into values in this world?

17. Did you expect Danny to run away?
    What makes his time on the streets tense and scary?

18. What insight into homelessness does Danny's time on the streets give you?

19. Nobody helps Danny during his time on the streets.
    Does this tell you anything about the society he is part of?

20. Would the story be very different if it were told from the point of view of Danny's father or mother?
    Use examples from the story to help explain your point of view.

21. Are you surprised that Andy woke up?
    How does his regaining consciousness impact on the story?
    How different would the story be if Andy did not wake up?

22. What is the mood like as the story ends?
    Can you explain what makes it this way?

23. What lesson does the author share with us in the novel?
    Is this a valuable lesson, do you think?

24. Describe the time and place this story is set in (the world of the novel).

What is appealing about this time and place?
What is unappealing about it?
Include examples in your answer.

25. What are the main themes/issues in this novel?
Explain your choices, using examples from the text.

26. What did you like about this novel?
Include examples in your answer.

27. What did you dislike about this novel?
Include examples in your answer.

28. Who is your favourite character?
What do you like and admire about them?

29. Which character do you dislike most?
Explain what makes you dislike them.

30. What different elements of the story combine to make this novel exciting?

31. Do you like the ending?
Does the ending complete the story?

32. Was there anything in the story that you would have liked to know more about?
Explain your answer fully, including examples.

33. Would this story make a good film?
What actors would you choose to play the key roles?
Explain your choices.

34. What was your favourite part of this story?
    Why did this section appeal to you?

35. Does this novel remind you of any other novels, films or television programmes?
    Explain your choices.

36. What design would you choose for the cover of this novel?
    Explain your choice of images.

37. Would you recommend this novel to a friend?
    Why/why not?

CLASSROOM QUESTIONS GUIDES

Books of questions, designed to save teachers time and lead to rewarding classroom experiences.

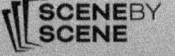

www.SceneBySceneGuides.com

www.ingramcontent.com/pod-product-compliance
Lightning Source LLC
Chambersburg PA
CBHW071035080526
44587CB00015B/2629